Time to listen, time to talk

John and Moyra Price

Falcon

First published 1973 in Australia as *Teenagers can be fun*
First published in UK 1974
Copyright © John and Moyra Prince 1974
Copyright for Appendix © Graham Cray
ISBN 0 85491 560 5
FALCON BOOKS
are published by Church Pastoral Aid Society,
Falcon Court, 32 Fleet Street, London EC4Y 1DB.
Not available for export.

Made and printed in Great Britain by
Hunt Barnard Printing Ltd., Aylesbury, Bucks.

Contents

Really so odd?

It is quite a number of years ago now, but the memory remains crystal clear. The two of us were staying with some close friends, and our host was ushering someone in to meet us. 'Come and meet', he said to them dramatically, 'some people who *enjoy* having two teenage children!'

That evening this book was conceived. Its antenatal life has been unnaturally long, but there are good reasons for that. At the time our second child was just 13, and it seemed even more impertinent to think of writing about parents and teenagers than it does now, when she and her elder brother are married, and the other two are 17 and 13 respectively.

However, let's get the record quite straight. This doesn't mean that we are setting ourselves up as the model parents of teenagers. We've made mistakes; we see some of them all too clearly now. Nor has it been plain sailing all the time. Far from it. Every family has its moments and we have certainly had ours. There have been tensions, too – *and* explosions. Ours is that kind of family – we are good at exploding. Yet somehow it has been and still is fun. Many parents could say the same, but this book is for those who find it just a bit traumatic to have teenage children.

Some time ago now our daughter, whose main mission in teenage life seemed to be to keep her father cut down to size, gave his ego one of the best boosts it ever received. In the course of a discussion about how best to help another family, she commented, 'But you're different, *we* talk.'

Surely she hit the nail right on its head. We have, on the whole, managed to keep our lines of communication open. Probably we all talk too much, but we do talk to each other – even if the other person isn't listening. So we can talk problems out. What is more, many issues never become problems; they remain issues to talk about.

How does one communicate with one's teenage children? That really is the key question and the one this book must try to answer. In fact, most of the book will be about communication in some way or other, or about the understanding without which communication is impossible.

One other introductory thing needs to be said. It is to sound a caution to convinced Christian parents who read this book. There are Christians who say, 'Our family life is quite secure. We pray for our children and commit their well-being to God. We know He can be relied upon to see that all will be well with our children.' Now we certainly do not decry either the value of prayer or the efficacy of faith. We write, in fact, as convinced Christians ourselves. But this approach is altogether too facile; there is a real sense in which God helps those who help themselves. In parenthood as elsewhere, He requires our conscious cooperation. We cannot simply offload by prayer the consequences of our own lack of effort or understanding. It is regrettably true that some of the most sincere Christian parents fail badly in their efforts to retain effective communication with their children.

Why this may be so we trust will emerge in what follows.

2 *Adolescence and the generation gap*

Adolescence

'Who invented this adolescence, anyway?' asked an irritated parent. 'Why can't children just grow into adults?'

The answers are fairly easy. Children do grow into adults but, in the western world as it now is, it takes time and that time is adolescence. When our ancestors ran about in woad there was no such thing. Once a child's body had grown strong enough and became sexually mature there was an initiation ceremony and, hey presto, the child was now an adult! There may have been a reluctant adult problem but adolescence didn't exist.

Adolescence – a transition stage between childhood and adulthood – is the product of a more sophisticated human society which demands long years of education to equip its members for adult life. In most developed western countries this transition period is still getting longer at both ends. Improved nutrition and health are causing children's bodies to mature ever earlier so that the onset of puberty is being advanced. At the same time education and vocational training become ever longer at the other end so that we no longer have an answer to the simple question, 'What is an adult?'

7

Picture the 16-year-old who lives away from home, earns his own living and virtually runs his life as he pleases, except that the law doesn't allow him to drive a car, vote, drink in a pub or marry without permission. Then take the 21-year-old student, living at home, still economically dependent on his parents to see him through. Which of the two enjoys more adult privileges? Add in all the possibilities between these two extremes and you have quite a muddle. The teenager doesn't know what he has to do to rate as an adult, the parent can't really tell him for the very good reason that society itself doesn't know.

So there is the adolescent, no longer a child in any way. In physique and sexual development his body is approaching maturity; socially his childish behaviour is a thing of the past; his interests and social inclinations are all but adult. Now he is ready to look at society and see what it expects of him. But which society should he look at? He can see at least four; one revealed by his own age group, a second represented by his parents and their 'old' friends, a third portrayed by the world of pop music and the glossy magazines (touches of the first are recognisable in this one). The fourth image is the most forbidding, the official society of authority whether at school, college, workshop or office. All four call for his allegiance and conformity and none of them agree about what he is to conform to!

Not, of course, that our adolescent works all this out consciously. He may not even find life all that confusing, expecially if he identifies himself strongly with one of these images of society and lets the others pass him by. On the other hand he may find some or all of the possible conflicts a real bother.

The generation gap

One thing is certain. Inside the home the considerable difference in outlook between the older and younger generations is sure to make itself felt. This generation gap is not new; the ancient Greeks knew all about it, for Plato complained about the youth of his day in strangely contemporary terms. There are two enduring sources of conflict between the old and the young in any changing society:

* The older generation has helped to make things the way they are and tends to see them as reasonably satisfactory, or a least as unavoidable. Youth sees change as both possible and necessary.

* The older generation feels the need to guide and control the younger; youth wants to be free to make its own decisions. The answer to the question 'When is someone grown-up?' will possibly always be 'About five years after he thinks he is and about five years before his parents think he is'!

It is hard to imagine society returning to such a static condition that these two sources of conflict would disappear. Then we have to add the differences of outlook which are the product of our particular age.

The parent generation today approaches life in ways that differ quite radically from those of our children. Here are some of the more obvious differences:

* We tend to *think* our way through problems by reasoning them out; they look for a solution that *feels* right regardless of what reasons they are given.

* We want to keep society stable and value respect for those in authority; they are much

more concerned about the liberty of the individual to run life as he wishes.

* We tend to be occupied with organisations and possessions; they with people and relationships.
* We are concerned with how other people see us, with the impression we are giving; they with how they actually are, regardless of the impression they give.
* We are concerned to safeguard the future. They tend to make the best of the present and let the future take care of itself.

These five points are a brief, almost crude, summary of the contrast between the rational approach of our scientific age and the non-rational post-scientific approach of our children. Readers wanting a fuller explanation of these differences will find further details in the appendix.

So where is the adolescent?

He is certainly caught in an awkward position. Under the influence of the pop culture and his friends, his outlook on life is gradually diverging from that of the adult world of his parents. But, as likely as not, his parents do not accept that he knows what life is about. So he feels that adult society won't accept him, though it constantly tells him to grow up and stop being a child. Inevitably he feels frustrated and insecure and takes refuge with other teenagers. They at least will accept him if he behaves as they do.

This power of the contemporaries group is one of the most obvious outward characteristics of teenage sub-culture. Hair and clothes must be worn in the same way that 'everybody does now', and so on. The whole life pattern seems to be dictated by the teenage group.

In fact the influence of the peer group is not nearly as great as many parents feel it to be. It shows up most strongly in what young people wear, how they speak and where they get together. These are relatively unimportant issues unless we make a major confrontation out of them. Sociologists are unanimous that by far the greatest influence on your teenage child is that of your own home. However, it is the *real* influence of the home, not the supposed or desired one, which reveals itself at this stage. One true story from a teaching career will illustrate. Working in an office behind a flimsy partition, a teacher in a public school heard this conversation between two boys.

'Say, Bob!'

'Yeah?'

'Why did your old man send you here?'

'Oh, come off it, Chris, where else?'

'Eh?'

'Well, the old man came here, and his old man and the one before that too.'

'Huh, I see – yeah, you couldn't really go anywhere else, could you?'

'That's right. Anyway, what about you, Chris?'

'Oh, I don't know. Sometimes I wonder why my old man spends all that bread.'

'Yes?'

'I've come to think that it must be to give me a bit of religion – but don't worry, Bob, what's good enough for Dad's good enough for me.'

In other words, the adolescent who has been encouraged to think independently by his school, his friends and the whole climate of opinion, begins to sift out your demands and instructions and to compare these with your behaviour. He questions the ban on smoking, when Dad lights up at will. He refuses to go to Sunday School any more if you never find it necessary to go to church. 'Do as I say' is no longer accepted and you have to settle for 'do as I do.' He finds it frustrating to have to submit to his parents' authority. 'Why should I do what they say? They don't even do it themselves!' is often a not unreasonable complaint.

There are other causes of frustration too, lying much deeper under the surface and much harder to overcome. We live in an age when almost everything comes to us in cans or plastic packs. Through the mass media, entertainment is also 'canned', while sport is often something to be watched rather than played. All this tends to give the teenager a secondhand experience of life, something vaguely flat and unsatisfying. He senses that life is failing to give him what it owes him, even though he cannot always say why he feels like this.

Furthermore he knows that he is better educated and informed than any previous generation of young people. Most probably he will end up pursuing his education well beyond that of his parents. He has views and wants to express them, but two things prevent him. The lack of firsthand experience of life makes it difficult for him to express just what he is trying to say, and when he does manage to be clear and articulate no one in the adult world wants to listen to him.

The Christian teenager from a typical church family is often particularly frustrated. He finds church adults inflexible, stuffy and out of touch with the normal current of teenage thinking. They, in turn, view him as rebellious and troublesome, which of course he may be.

The teenage period is not necessarily a troublesome period, though it certainly is a time of uncertainty and insecurity, a time when young people need understanding. Parents sometimes complain of the lack of consideration their teenage children give them. 'They should try to understand *our* point of view' we have heard them say. Surely this is topsy-turvy. It is the parents who are adult and, one hopes, mature. If understanding is to be shown between parents and teenagers it must start on the parents' side They must show understanding of and to their children – only then can they hope for understanding in return.

3 *The typical teenager*

Is there such a person as a typical teenager? Fortunately not! Human beings are all different; delightfully, excitingly and, at times exasperatingly, different. No one fits the 'average' pattern perfectly. But the pattern is useful all the same, because it gives us an idea of some of the things we may expect in that teenage son or daughter in our home.

The teenager's needs

The basic needs of the adolescent are pretty obvious and can be summed up by saying that youth needs to find solutions to the problems of life. There is nothing new in that. What is new is that the main problems of life have shifted to the emotional and social realm. It is problems of relationships that loom largest for young people today. They want to get on well with others.

In view of this, *emotional support*, which all human beings need, is particularly important for teenagers today. They need to be loved, respected and accepted in their own right, particularly at home. 'Of course our children can rely on the support of our home,' may be your quick reaction. No doubt this is true. In the face of a major crisis most of us would certainly stand behind our children, but when there is no crisis to weld us together it is so easy to take each other for granted and go our own selfish ways. We parents get absorbed in our adult affairs and don't find the time for the family that we should. When we are at home the television set prevents us talking to our children so that, without meaning to, we actually give them little attention. As a result many teenagers do not find their basic needs of acceptance and support met within their homes.

Instead they seek this acceptance in a like-minded group of friends. Do not let us resent this group too much. It fulfils a necessary and important function, and where the home provides the needed underlying support its influence will not be unduly great. If the home fails, then the teenager will have an exaggerated need for the support of the peer group, and may be undesirably swayed by it because it is all that he has to hang on to.

At first sight it may seem strange that one source of emotional security and of a sense of acceptance is a growing *feeling of independence*, particularly in the economic and social spheres of life. There is something rather pathetic about the fussing parent whose adolescent child 'has never spent a night away from our roof.' Such overprotection keeps a teenager in a child's position. A child is dependent, an adult is independent and an adolescent must be given the satisfaction of steadily growing independence, without being left feeling totally unsupported.

The satisfaction which comes from meeting the challenges of independence successfully will lead the teenager towards *the full life*, to which, deep down, he aspires. Life begins to be worthwhile and full in another sense too. Before our daughter's marriage we used to find ourselves quite exhausted by the hectic whirl of social and religious activities which our three teenagers managed to cram into one short weekend. If you have normal teenagers in your home you will know all about this too. They have an enormous zest for life, these teenagers of ours, and they use that zest to live that life to the very fullest.

This is partly because they are proving to themselves that life has meaning. They are finding that meaning in the experience of social intercourse. By making a niche in a circle of friends they are finding their identity, they are finding purpose and meaning in life. What if, as a result, they do fail exams? That is surely, so they feel, quite secondary to the real business of living life.

Teenagers today are looking for solutions to the problems of life, particularly on the emotional and social level; they have a great need for the emotional security of being truly loved, respected and accepted; they want to achieve a feeling of independence, without being left to cope entirely alone. In these and other ways they want to find purpose and the achievement of leading a full life.

Problems

Though the problems of teenagers are many and varied, these problems fall into a few broad groups. In a recent Australian survey, it was found that right at the top of all the problem lists, for boys and girls, younger and older, whether at school or not, were the 'rat-race' problems. They worried most about exams, about not doing well at a job or at school. Failure leads to non-acceptance at school or at work, to disapproval at home, and possibly to lowered esteem among the group. The drop-out group naturally arises as a defence against this disapproval.

Problems of social relationships came second on the list. 'How to behave with the opposite sex' worried boys at school almost as much as the rat-race problems, though girls found this less worrying. Very few complained of not having enough friends, though many said that having plenty of friends was the most important thing in life. This suggests that young people today handle relationships with their friends and acquaintances with considerable poise.

On the other hand, they find home relationships much harder to handle. A quarter of all the young people were bothered about unhappiness at home. Whether real or imagined, these difficulties loom equally large for the products of all kinds of homes, irrespective of age, but a little more largely for girls than for boys. Home relationships are not just social but also involve questions of authority, and individual freedom. This makes them much more difficult, both for the teenagers and for the older generation who don't really see why young people so resent authority and so want freedom. Yet is it important to understand their concern.[1] We shall stand alongside them much more easily when we understand why they feel as they do.

Moral issues are also a considerable problem to young people. The opposite sex question is obviously a moral as well as a social one, but it would be quite wrong to limit teenage moral problems to the areas of sex, drink and drugs. In fact they are very concerned too with how people treat each other. They see honesty and kindness as important and despise the insincerity and self-seeking of many of their elders. All these moral issues have a common slant. Young people today tend to work from an emotional sense of

[1] See Appendix.

what they feel to be moral. If morality is to make life more meaningful, more worth living, it must make the teenager *feel right*.

Although moral issues are very important, teenagers do not press earnestly and consistently towards resolving them. Rather the opposite. A moral issue is grappled with just while circumstances force attention on it and, if circumstances make the problem less urgent, then it will be left to slide till it becomes urgent again. Thus the quest for moral solutions is a haphazard one – as circumstances happen to dictate.

The same is true of finding the point of life. The teenager approaches this as a personal quest rather than an intellectual one. If the teenager asks 'Why am I here?' he does not mean 'What is the rational explanation for my being here?' His question is more nearly 'What am I going to do with life, seeing I've got it?' It's a problem of identity and purpose.

We see then four general areas in which young people have problems – the rat race, attitudes to authority, the moral sphere and the meaning of life. This may not cover everything, but most of the more common problems fall in one of these four broad categories.

Interests

At the top of the poll of interests in the Australian survey were 'the opposite sex' (boys) and 'how you look and dress' (girls). Hardly surprising! 'Sport' and 'going out' rated highly. Work or study, hobbies and reading books were well down the list with, to our surprise, television. Favourite evening activities included the rather vague 'getting with the group' and 'relaxing with a friend'. The main thing for young people is to be with others. What they do while they are together is of secondary importance. They just want to be with the group.

It is not surprising therefore that the formal activities of youth clubs find little support. In the survey only about one in eight said they enjoyed youth club activities. Socials and dances were also much less popular than 'visiting a friend', while a 'party' was the favourite youth activity. Older teenagers, particularly, greatly prefer informal activities with no organised programme structure.

Today's young people, then, are strongly orientated towards the social side of life. They are, on the whole, fortunate in having many social outlets and they handle quite well the relationships involved in them. They usually choose friends who see things as they do, so that our children's friends commonly reflect the set of values that our home has passed on to our children.

It is most important that we, the parents, should recognise the importance of our children's social needs. Let's make our homes places where their friends are obviously welcome, even if the horde takes over the living room and we end up in the kitchen. When coffee gets spilt on the best carpet, or the wall plaster gets chipped or the paper scarred, our system of values is challenged. Is the home there to be kept looking nice, or is it a place to be lived in and used? Our teenagers have no doubt about the answer. They aren't out to wreck the place but possessions are for using, even if they do incur wear and tear. Sure, there have to be some limits, but be careful how you insist on them.

We are not suggesting that our children be given

their heads and allowed to run not only their own lives but ours, and our homes, exactly as they wish. Provided they feel they are being given real understanding, most teenagers are extraordinarily sensible. It is neither a case of 'giving in to them all along the line', nor of 'laying down the law with an iron hand', but of dealing with each issue sensitively and sensibly.

In summary, then, the teenager is not basically different from other human beings, though his transition situation tends to make him feel more insecure. Recognising this insecurity, we should appreciate his need to be respected and accepted as the growingly independent individual he aspires to be. Just as it is a mistake to treat a young child as a miniature adult, so it is mistaken to treat an adolescent as just an older child. He is that, but no more than he is a younger adult. The more he is treated as an adult, the sooner he will truly become one.

4 _How the teenager ticks_

Is the average teenager so bad? Worse than we were at his age? Or better? Sociologists and theologians would probably agree, for quite different reasons, that we are all basically similar human material, but that they in the seventies are moulded a little differently from the teenagers of the thirties, forties and fifties. Different, but neither worse nor better.

Permissive?

One of the pleasing and hopeful things about today's young people is that they are more truly tolerant than we knew how to be. They are not tolerant just because they do not care; they care very much about many things. But today's emphasis on the freedom of the individual makes it easier to accept another person 'doing his own thing', even if in doing it he acts in ways we would never think of doing. This commendable tolerance, tolerance on principle, is a refreshing contrast with the narrow conformity into which we in our youth were often forced, before we in turn forced the next school generation into our mould with equal dedication.

Of course this coin of tolerance has another side which is not so easy to accept. If we tolerate the person who is different, we permit him to live and act as he wishes, and so youth today is permissive as well as tolerant. But a caution – the word 'permissive' has almost come to mean 'licentious' or 'immoral'. It doesn't really mean this. It merely means that we permit others to act according to their own moral dictates, without trying to make them conform to ours, either by law or some other form of pressure. In this sense many young people are permissive, though this does not mean that they approve of what others do. Far from it. They may well regard the conduct of others as stupid and disapprove strongly, but they will probably try to understand the other person's motives rather than condemn him.

It is possible to confuse this permissive, non-condemning outlook with a lack of definite moral convictions. On the whole this would be a mistake. Young people in today's western society have great freedom of moral choice, possibly more than ever before due to the declining cohesion of society as a whole. Yet the great majority seem to use their freedom most responsibly, showing that they have a well-developed moral sense. Parents who trust their children will find their trust is usually not misplaced. Others show up less well: the untrusted often prove untrustworthy; the uncared-for use their freedom to kick back at the uncaring adult world, while some simply misuse their human freedom of choice for no apparent reason other than that they are children of Adam and Eve!

Undisciplined?

Tolerance and permissiveness leads us to the subject of discipline, unquestionably one of the 'outest' of out words with youth today. Young people do not take easily to 'good old-fashioned discipline', laid down with a heavy hand from above. They rebel against it and are often smart enough to turn the tables on their blustering elders when they produce a confrontation. This objection to authoritarian control is not really indiscipline so much as a natural striving for independence, a development we shall consider in chapter 6.

Discipline is a more personal quality and not one in which today's youth excels. For example, many fail to settle down to the hard grind of study because it does not seem to be leading them anywhere – towards their own goals in life, that is. Grind for grind's sake is pointless, they feel, and, lacking the motivation which a clear goal gives, they appear lazy and undisciplined. But let something motivate them, then their grit and determination becomes admirable. The difficulty is that their self-discipline is often called for by goals which seem of little importance to us, the parents. It all comes down to the question of aims, and on this subject each generation finds it hard to agree that the other may be right.

Generally speaking, at their age, we were happy to work hard to qualify ourselves for a job, a good income and security. Some of us were more ambitious and set out to get to the top. Now our teenagers look at us and wonder whether our approach unlocked the secrets of life for us. Often they doubt whether it did. They also see, or hear of, the frustration of university students with their irrelevant and unsatisfying courses and naturally they question whether the long hard grind is going to be worthwhile. Life may well unlock its secrets without this, though they really have only the haziest ideas as to how this may happen.

So we find ourselves complaining with some justification that young people today won't stick at things. This characteristic, call it weakness if you like, has another cause too. Teenagers today have grown up in an age of prosperity. They have not experienced the struggle for simple necessities which helps to teach persistence. If anything their problem is the other way – how to get satisfaction out of a life which gives too much too easily – and this explains some of the teenager's frustration.

Materialistic? Idealistic?

On the whole young people today are not material-istic. To them people matter more than things, and this is good. The older generation will reply, 'It's easy not to be materialistic when you've got everything you want.' Again, largely true. It is easy for each generation to find fault with the other and fail to see its good qualities. Young people see how preoccupied with material possessions their elders have become and react against the qualities of hard work and thrift. On the other hand, older people criticise the irres-ponsibility and improvidence of youth, without giving sufficient credit for youth's scale of values which restores people to their proper place in relation to material things.

Rather than argue the relative merits of the two viewpoints, the important thing is to recognise their deep differences. Parents cannot expect to force their children into their own mould. We have to pass on a basic attitude of responsibility, which the younger generation has to work out in its own way.

The question of materialism is perhaps linked with that of the supposed 'idealism' or 'altruism' of youth. Is youth idealistic? In one important sense the answer must be an enduring yes. Youth has life in front of it and needs ideals to tell it where to head. Life has not yet blunted this idealism by revealing how hard it is to maintain or achieve our ideals. Thus youth is idealistic, while older people regard themselves as more realistic. The difference is due to a simple unchanging fact – older people have lived longer than younger ones!

But the word 'idealism' is often used in a rather different and technically less correct sense, to mean the opposite of self-interest, an idea which is more correctly conveyed by the term 'altruism'. Are young people today particularly altruistic, particularly disinterested and unselfish? Undoubtedly many of them would like to think they are, but we fear the facts do not support them. The survey showed that young people on the whole seem little concerned with the social ills around them, except where they are directly involved themselves. Essentially their altruism is the same as other people's; it is called forth by personal involvement.

5 *Lines of communication*

'Well, I've got a teenage child now, I suppose I'd better start learning how to communicate with him.' This parent has not only left it too late; he probably does not really understand what communication is. It is not something to start at adolescence or any other stage of life. Communication is a basic element in human relationships, achieved by actions and gestures as well as by words. Some would go so far as to say that communication *is* the relationship, that without it there simply is no such thing as a relationship. They may be playing a little with words but they do make a vital point. We express relationships by communication with people, and a relationship which is not expressed is of little value; effectively it does not exist. In this sense some husbands have no relationship with their wives and some parents do not relate to their children.

Good communication is therefore basic to any human relationship and, unfortunately, it is seriously lacking in many modern homes. What is more, many families accept the poor communication they experience as normal and don't realise that change is possible. Yet the communication pattern in a home does not remain static. Good communication may deteriorate for some reason, while poor communication can be improved, though this improvement is not easy to bring about quickly. This possibility of improvement is there for parents who realise that they are in the 'late start' category. We shall think about that situation a little later, but first let us ask how we may develop desirable communication patterns in the home in the first place.

The simple answer is 'by being all that parents should be from the very beginning', an ideal goal none of us goes near to achieving. However, the answer implies a most important point of principle. The initiative for relationships and communication in the home belongs to the parents. Parents who blame their children for the fact that 'they never talk to us' have the whole thing wrong. It isn't even a question of who *ought* to initiate communication; it is a question of who *can*.

As parents we have to accept that the whole initiative for communication rests with ourselves, not just as a question of responsibility but as a matter of fact. It is we who taught our children to talk and thus equipped them with the most essential means of human communication. At this stage communication probably began quite well. It is such an exciting part of childhood and we all enjoy our children's early adventures in speech. That is the trap. Beginnings are exciting; the subsequent slow growth is not and it takes time and trouble.

Time – this is probably the crux of the problem. It takes time to develop those early seeds of communication into a relationship big enough to carry through the years. It does not matter much what we do with the children in that time; what is important is that we are available to them. There may be little talking but shared experiences provide the essential soil in which relationships grow and in which discussion and the sharing of ideas can naturally take place.

Do not picture the ideal family as a kind of miniature parliament – a talking shop where someone is always discussing something really important. There may be homes of this intensely stimulating kind, but they are rare enough to be regarded as highly desirable oddities! In the normal home with good family communications, discussion of serious issues probably occupies a very small proportion of the time of any member of the family. But the point is that such discussion does occur and it occurs naturally and spontaneously, not usually because someone sets out to start a discussion, but because it just happened. It happened because parents and children were open to each others' ideas and also because they were available – they had time.

We all know how ineffective it is when father clears his throat and says, 'Now I want to talk to you, my boy'. It just doesn't work. It doesn't work because it is artificial, whereas good communication is natural. It doesn't work because it almost invites resistance to what is about to be imposed. There are certainly times when parents, and perhaps particularly father, have to take a direct initiative in tackling a family problem, or an individual child's problem. If the problem is very urgent a natural opportunity almost inevitably presents itself. If it doesn't, one can usually get discussion started without a frontal attack. When the problem is less urgent it nearly always pays to wait till you find yourself talking to the teenager. You may have to take the initiative to raise what is on your mind but this is different from 'sailing in cold' with the ominous warning, 'I want to talk to you.'

The background to sound patterns of communication, then, is one of time spent with the children, of interest taken in their activities. Stories at bedtime when younger, sporting fixtures attended later on, picnics and outings shared, help given with homework and projects, interesting books passed on, films seen and talked about, all these and many others are grist to the mill of building family relationships. Holidays also have a key place because time is more freely available to us all then and because we are sharing the pleasure and excitement of different activities in a different place.

Perhaps too we do not share our family affairs sufficiently. Is it really so dreadful that our children know how much or how little money we have? Do they really have to be excluded from decisions about the family future? That new job, for example, may involve them all in new schools, and perhaps they have as much right to share in the discussion as anyone. But regardless of right, their views are often a real help in arriving at the best decision and there is no doubt that family communication benefits greatly when major issues affecting the family are discussed together.

Some years ago we experienced a sudden change in our family situation. A quite unexpected, rather traumatic, parting with what had looked like a worthwhile job for years to come meant a complete upheaval for the family. Inevitably we all talked about the future together, at great length, over quite a long period. One day our rather sensitive number three said, 'You know, I'd like us to do something really interesting, like going to New Guinea or somewhere really different.' None of us for a moment dreamed that his words would prove prophetic, but they certainly made it much easier to face boarding schools and other drastic changes when in fact we did go off to New Guinea. Rather than weakening our family ties the decision, with its resulting separations, seemed to cement them.

Two other areas of family communication are so important that each will require a chapter of its own. Hang-ups over sex tend to carry across to the whole field of more delicate personal problems, whereas the freedom to discuss these things may well unlock other doors and make children feel that they can discuss the most sensitive and personal things with their parents.

Religion too can be a great help or serious hindrance to home relationships. The family that really prays together does seem to stay together. Religious experiences are very personal and sharing them often opens up communication at a particularly intimate level. However, there can be a much less favourable other side. Children who are reluctantly acquiescent in their parents' religious life in childhood often come to feel, when they begin to make their own decisions in adolescence, that they do not share their parents' devotion. What could have been a means of particularly good communication then becomes a most serious obstacle.

All that we have said so far has been by way of general principle, applying in some form throughout childhood and on up into adolescence. It would truly be a paragon of a parent who put all these things into practice all the time. In fact, children are wonderfully resilient creatures. As parents we fail them constantly. Sometimes temporary harm seems to be done but they bounce back quickly and tolerate many of the idiosyncracies of their 'troublesome' parents with much endurance. It is the underlying attitude of parents that is the crucial thing. This *has* to be right.

6 *Keeping the lines open*

'Jenny, where are you?'

'Here dear, what's the matter, Ralph?'

'That rig-out of Tim's – have you seen it?'

'Yes, dear.'

'Well?'

'He didn't make a very wise choice, I'm afraid.'

'Not a very wise choice! Are you being deliberately funny? If he'd ransacked the city for the most unsuitable combination of shirt and tie to go with his trousers, he couldn't have done better anywhere. I've told him so – in no uncertain terms.'

'You haven't!'

'And, what's more, I've told him that if he's going to spend his whole allowance on stuff like that, he can go back to 50p a week pocket money.'

'Poor Tim!' sighed mother.

Yes, poor Tim! After getting himself square with his first monthly allowance, he's had such fun launching out with his second. He wasn't quite sure how he'd survive the next four weeks on 76 pence, but it would be worth it. Just wait till the kids at Friday night saw that tie. Oh boy! And then Dad had bust the whole thing. He'd actually stuffed the tie in his wastepaper basket after Dad's blast – but later he fished it out, a little crushed, and straightened it out. As he soothed its crushed fibres, his crushed pride recovered very little. Certainly one thing was made very clear by this very first experience of doing what he really wanted with his allowance. He'd make jolly sure Dad never found out again what he did with it. And he'd die rather than let Dad know he was short of a few pence at the end of the month. Yes, he'd die first, poor Tim!

Poor Ralph, rather, and Jenny too! Their communication with Tim had not been wonderful during earlier years, but it hadn't been very poor either. Things had been a bit more difficult since Tim went to secondary school. It was to try and make him a bit more responsible and to stop him always wanting a bit for this and a bit for that that Ralph had just recently given him an allowance, telling him he could do anything he liked with it as long as he didn't come back and ask for more before the end of the month. It had really done wonders too. Tim had been most responsible with his first allowance and he'd been most helpful in other ways around the place too. He'd even begun to open up about school a bit now and then. But Ralph had rather spoilt that now.

A true story? It could be, and it serves well enough to illustrate the next key point. Early and mid-adolescence is the time when earlier good relationships may be seriously damaged, and when parents can lose altogether what little communication they did have with their children in earlier years. It is a very sensitive period and one in which everything depends upon how parents handle their children's growing independence. The personal maturity of parents is now on trial. Do we really want our children to develop into independent personalities, or are we, deep down, trying to keep them dependent on ourselves? Do we want to perpetuate them as our children, or are we really looking forward to the day when these teenagers will be our equals in the adult world?

If we are progressively welcoming them to the adult circle, we shall find that a great deal of ourselves brushes off on our children – our strong points, our weaknesses and even our idiosyncrasies. Mothers with good taste produce daughters who seem to know what is fitting, without particularly trying to do so. Sons naturally follow their father's interests and inclinations. Many of the transitions towards adulthood in fact proceed quite naturally and easily.

Nevertheless there will be tension. The stable relationship we had with our children when they were younger is undergoing major changes, and all of us find the changes hard to adapt to. We shall relax a great deal of the tension if, as parents, we welcome the first signs of independence because they tell us that our teenagers are maturing. It is a good thing that they want to argue with us, not now in the childish arguments of disobedience, but seriously expressing their views. It is good that they begin to want to do things a little differently from the way we do them. It is good that they begin to want to wear their own style of clothes and their hair differently from the way older people do.

Of course these first signs of independence will be rather gauche. A baby's first steps are terribly uncertain. Any moment the law of gravity will take over. But we don't push him over; we give him a helping hand. The adolescent's first experiments in independence are equally insecure. He is very self-conscious and sensitive to criticism. Ridicule or sarcasm can deliver an emotional body blow which does lasting damage to the parent-child relationship. He needs the helping hand of encouragement above all else at this time. Yet something in us tends to make us withhold this. Psychologists explain that we see our growing children as a threat to our adult security so we discourage them. Perhaps that is so, though it is not how mature people should act. This is the stage where the adolescent needs the helping hand towards maturity.

So look forward to the opportunity which these first signs of independence offer. The whole future communication pattern with our teenage child is at stake. Encourage his growing independence; listen to his views; let him do things his own way. Of course his views will be immature; how could they be anything else? Yet they are put forward seriously and deserve to be treated seriously. Of course their proposed change to our way of doing things is sometimes slow and inefficient. Does that matter? The point is that it is their own, not ours. Of course some of the clothes, make-up and hair styles may be unsuitable, extravagant or downright bad taste. But what if money has been wasted, in one sense? In another it has been well spent buying experience.

In order to be able to develop independence the adolescent needs to know where he or she stands. For instance, a teenager should normally be given an allowance of money and it must be quite clear just what this is meant to cover; the more independence it can give the better. We have never been in a position to give our children more than a very modest sum, but it has been quite clear that it has to cover everything except school clothes, and that they are free to spend it as they like. This policy expands school uniform remarkably but otherwise it works very well! Having made such arrangements, our itchy parental hands have to be totally removed. Of course we see waste, unwise spending and so on. But we try not to interfere. It is independence we are trying to teach.

It is not always possible to spell things out quite so clearly. One cannot say, 'you are now fourteen, you can discuss with me whether to go to scouts, or which way to mow the lawn, but not whether you come to church or not'. Such things are determined by the present state of the developing relationship. Generally, when the adolescent feels able to discuss something, then that is the right and proper time for that topic to be reasonably debated between parent and child.

We should, then, welcome and encourage signs of independence, even though our first reaction is to find them trying, even irritating. We do not have to approve of everything, but there are better ways of moulding people than by criticising directly the things of which we disapprove. It is much more effective to comment 'I like that!' when teenage daughter appears tastefully dressed than to tear apart the unfortunate get-up that she probably realises herself hasn't really come off.

Expressing appreciation is a nice habit we all too rarely practise. One sometimes wonders why, because it produces such a response. Within the home we all tend to take others far too much for granted – parents each other, children their parents and parents their children as much as any. After all, it's only the family, so there's no need to ask if we can borrow something or to say 'thank you' when we have. We don't bother to pass the butter or say 'Excuse me please' when we leave the table. And we certainly don't tell them how good they are; they might get swelled heads. Or is it just that we don't bother? Yet the sense of being appreciated works magic with communication. We all respond to people who appreciate us, and our teenagers are no exception.

Saying sorry is as important as saying thank you. We may be parents, but we are not right all the time. We make lots of mistakes, we get angry, we are thoughtless; we admit it to our friends readily enough. But not to our children; oh no! What on earth would they think of us if we climbed down to them? The answer is only too simple. Respect is lost by covering up, never by putting a wrong right. Of course they should learn to apologise when they need to, but what better way to teach them than by showing that we can do so too. Such a mutual sincerity really helps communication.

Of course all this is really only part of love in action. Loving one another means more than having an emotional feeling. It means expressing appreciation; it means saying sorry; it means giving understanding; it means having time for people; it means being willing to listen and it means many other things. Remember that communication is a two-way thing; we tend to make it a one-way process – from parent to child. Actually the other direction is really more important, but it is also out of our control. We can decide when we will talk but not when they will. If only our teenagers would talk to us when it's convenient for us – but they don't.

Bob can tell when he collects Peter off the late train that he's got something on his mind.

'Had a good day, Pete?'

'All right, thanks, Dad.'

'Anything interesting?'

'Not really.'

Bob drives on in a heavy silence.

'Something on your mind, Pete?'

'Nope.'

Silence engulfs them again till home looms up. Peter disappears to his room to emerge minimally for tea. Two hours later, when Bob is in the middle of adding up a column of figures in his tax return, Peter bursts in.

'Dad?'

'Yes?'

'What am I going to do about . . . ?'

Bob heaves an inward sigh, forgets about the tax return and listens to the problem he knew was there as soon as Peter came off the train. But he was wise. Peter would only discuss it when he felt ready, and that was when he would have to listen.

For us this is both the cross and the great joy of being the parents of teenage children. We know of a couple who have had to get a larger bed, because they – and their teenagers – have gone through three in the course of their Friday night sessions! It so happens that this is a habit of our family's too. They have been much addicted to the church's Friday night youth club. Some time between 10.30 and 11.30 they come in and usually we are in bed by that time. One of them pokes his head round the door. Father pretends to be more asleep than he is, but the news of the evening just won't keep and the first invader is inside the room.

'Mummy, guess what happened tonight!'

Father pulls the blankets further up as number one plunges on the bed beside him. He knows that it is only a matter of minutes before all three will be spreadeagled all over the bed and him, and sleep will be banished. Oh well, he doesn't have to get up early in the morning, but why didn't we invest in a bigger bed too?

Actually these Friday night bed fellowship sessions

in our house have been a wonderful channel of communication. They just happened, of course – no one thought them up. No one could think up anything so ridiculous as two parents under the bedclothes and three large rumbustious teenagers rolling round above the bedclothes, all competing for bed space. It would have been very easy, especially for early-go-to-bed father, to have choked them off. It was late-go-to-bed mother, rather than conscientious parenthood, which allowed it to develop. But we learned a valuable lesson. Let the kids talk when they want or they won't talk at all.

Of course all this is costly, of our time particularly. It is a nuisance constantly to have to put aside what one wants to do at that moment, be it study, tax returns or sleep. But the results repay the cost many times over.

Without warning at the end of the whole process something very exciting happens. Some question arises; your son decides firmly and irrevocably that he is leaving school, or your far-too-young 18-year-old daughter wants to get engaged. The request is couched most respectfully and courteously; there is no putting a pistol at your head. But behind the approach the impression is inescapable. Your teenage child is looking you in the face from your own level and discussing the question with you as an equal, with the firmness of a new maturity. At first it is a bit of a shock. Yet it is at the same time rather delightful – you are dealing with an adult. Your child really has grown up!

7 *Clearing the blocks*

All this is fine for the parents whose children are still young. They still have time to prepare for the future adolescence of their children. But what about Ralph and Jenny and their ilk, the ones who are only waking up now to the facts that they have teenage children, that they really should have started years ago, that the lines of communication are hopelessly blocked or simply do not exist? Is it altogether too late, or can something still be done? The answer, of course, is that it is only too late to tackle a problem when the problem has ceased to be. But the longer the problem is left, the less may be achieved and the harder it will be to achieve anything. If communication is lacking at the beginning of adolescence it can be started, but it will not be easy to start it from scratch naturally. It certainly will not just happen of its own accord. Parents have to do the starting – but how?

Family communication is one of these cases where being aware of a difficulty is halfway to overcoming it, but only halfway. Living together in a home provides so many little opportunities of interaction that effective communication may follow just because you are aware of the need for it. It will only do so, however, if you seize your opportunities. The initiative is in your hands; you must use it and use it naturally. A blatant change of approach raises, consciously or unconsciously, the reaction, 'Hullo! What's this for? What's coming now?' The teenager is on his guard, watchful and tense and quite unlikely to be receptive. You will only get through to your teenagers in circumstances which enable them to be relaxed and natural. Anything forced or artificial altogether prevents this.

Communication, as we have seen, is much more than conversation or discussion. These form a part of communication, but discussion at any depth will only occur where effective communication already exists. This is the trouble with the 'Now my boy, I want to talk to you' approach. It seems to assume that you can just open a tap on demand and make effective communication occur. Nothing could be further from the truth. If your children are to discuss their problems with you, then lines of communication must already exist. These lines can be developed in a variety of ways, all of which involve sharing activities and interests together.

Fortunately for the late-start parent, there are a lot of activities which it is perfectly natural to initiate early in adolescence. The beginning of secondary school marks a point where it is quite natural to become much more interested in homework, though obviously this needs care. There is such a fine line between being willing to help when there is difficulty and breathing down the neck of a reluctant recipient of attention. Don't nag about homework, don't make it a bone of contention – not if it can be avoided. The balance is a delicate one, but rightly held, homework and school generally can provide a way of being fruitfully involved with your teenage children's life.

Sport provides another possible link between parents and teenage children. Circumstances vary so much from family to family that it is very difficult to generalise. In some families it may be the youth club, or some other hobby activity that takes the place of the sporting team. The exact nature of the activity really does not matter at all. It is the fact that you are sharing in your children's interest that is important. Inevitably this involves time.

There are no ways of clearing the lines that do not involve time. The short cuts simply do not work. One teenager put it brutally frankly when he blurted out in bitter anger, 'The trouble is that Dad thinks he can buy me; well, he just can't!' He was reacting violently to a very common mistake of busy but wealthy parents. They think they can make up for the lack of time they give to their children by giving them the most lavish presents. The sad thing is that the more the teenager is given the less he tends to respond to the giver. Time may be money, but in the matter of relationships money certainly is not time.

At the other end of the scale, some parents make money a total barrier between themselves and their children, simply by failing to provide even the essential minimum which their children need. We have heard parents say, 'We house, feed and clothe our children, we pay their fares and give them their collection money – what do they need money for?' The result is constant mortification for their children, who cannot accept the gift of a single piece of chocolate because they know they can never return it. This is the kind of home where definite steps need to be taken to give teenage children the necessary financial independence. Those steps alone will not open up communication, but they may remove a major obstacle to it.

Unreasonable restriction on children's social life, or on their freedom to choose their friends, is another obstacle to communication. Obvious – and easily said. It is not so easy to answer the question – what is 'unreasonable'? Some practical suggestions will be included when we discuss the general question of social life in chapter 9, but the point here is that unreasonable control will be a block between parents and children. Somewhat surprisingly, unduly lax control has the same effect, because it conveys the impression that parents do not care.

Quite often a block between parents and their teenage children is the result of a number of points of tension which are in themselves all quite trivial. Disputes over clothes or hair styles, the volume of the radio or the selection of the television programmes can easily be built up into a major confrontation. Sometimes this is because as parents we have been so used to dictating the terms to our younger children that we have, unconsciously, become much more selfish than we realise. This may be difficult to admit, but it is fairly easy to remedy once we bring ourselves to do so.

It may be the other way round, too. If we have been over-indulgent to our children, we may have made them unduly selfish and demanding and this may be much more difficult to correct. A stand-up row will not achieve anything. There are occasions when parents do have to talk straight to their teenagers, and usually this will be accepted or even appreciated as long as the approach is not entirely one-sided. We shall not succeed, however, by pious talk or laying down the law, in covering up our hypocrisy or selfishness. Confrontation and broken communication inevitably result.

We have found that we need a lot of self-control and sober judgment, often more than we have been able to muster at the time. Perhaps we have been worked up by somebody's comment. We really can't have people thinking *that* about our children, and so we go off half-cock. Result – blow-up, hurt feelings and, at least temporarily, one uptight teenager. When the two of us have disciplined ourselves to stop and think, to talk over the problem together and work out a way of handling it, it has always worked out much better. Often the difficulty solved itself without our intervention. When something had to be said, it could be said much more calmly and acceptably as the result of a little reflection.

There are then two ways in which communication has to be worked at by parents who feel out of touch with their teenage children. The positive aspect involves building lines of communication with them by sharing their activities and interests. The negative side involves removing obstacles as far as possible and preventing further blocks developing.

The most important thing of all is that our teenage children must feel they are trusted. Distrust is the most irremovable obstacle in any line of communication. Now this can be very difficult indeed. For you cannot screw yourself up to say 'I trust you' where distrust exists. Once you have made it clear, by word or action, that you do not trust your children, it is very hard indeed to reverse the situation. Ideally, mutual trust has to be built up in earlier years and allowed to develop naturally as the child grows older.

Adolescence provides many opportunities for demonstrating increasing trust in your children, so that any sense of suspicion and distrust is dispelled. It opens up a whole range of new responsibilities which can be used to develop mutual trust and respect. Baby-sitting younger brothers and sisters instead of being baby-sat, coping with visitors until we can get home, a long journey unaccompanied and unsupervised, or permission to take the car out are just a few of the more obvious ways of demonstrating that we accept our teenagers as responsible near-equals.

There is a chicken-and-egg relationship between the trust we place in someone and their trustworthiness. The ideal we all hope for runs round a circle. We help our children develop a sound moral sense, so they can be trusted; we therefore trust them and they honour our trust in them; having proved them trustworthy we trust them further. The responsibility thus placed upon them draws the best from them . . . and so on back round the circle. Unfortunately there is a similar much less desirable, indeed vicious, circle which can also develop. Somewhere along the line we find a teenager untrustworthy and he knows it. We are reluctant to risk being let down again and awareness of this further undermines our relationship, thus causing lack of trust to increase untrustworthiness further. How is this situation to be avoided?

None of us can expect that our teenagers will never let us down. They are, after all, our own very human children and we shall need to deal with failure carefully when it occurs. It is very tempting to drive home the line, 'I'm shocked that a child of mine could have let me down so badly' when really nothing needs to be said at all. The sense of guilt and failure is almost certainly causing the teenager deep pain, and the fact that his parents know what has happened is sufficient punishment and corrective. At these times restraint is likely to produce more respect and response than rebuke. Handled rightly a case of breach of trust can be a great teacher, but handled unfeelingly and mercilessly it can turn relations very sour. This is just one more delicate balance which we, as parents, have to find.

Trust has to be mutual and it normally requires mutual respect. Real respect is not based on fear but on admiration for the qualities of the other person, and this respect has to be *earned*. Our present ideas of respect have changed a great deal from the old Victorian image of respect for parents, which really could amount to a total absence of real relationships. One of our sons currently delights in the admonition 'Bag your head, father dear!' Is he being disrespectful, or actually demonstrating his respect?

8 *Your child . . . or himself?*

Independence, making their own decisions. Allowing our children these things is not enough; we must actively help them to become independent. Obviously this means that we must trust them, but that is not all. We must also aim to set them up to live their own lives, rather than to be reflections of ourselves, our aims, or our thwarted ambitions.

Some parents do deliberately plan their children's careers for them. Having decided on the goal, they consciously press their children towards it because they see it as part of their parental duty to do so. 'He'll appreciate what I did for him when he's older,' is the line used to cover up the almost total lack of communication which often results. History suggests that 'he' rarely does!

But most of us try not to be like this – not consciously, that is. We probably restrain ourselves, most of the time, from nagging about study and aims in life. Unconsciously, though, there is inevitably something of the ambitious parent in all of us. It is only natural. We have experienced enough of life to have clear ideas about how our children will get the best out of life. This 'best way' may be a particular career which has given us great satisfaction, or one we always aspired to but never attained; it may be simply an academic qualification with its prestige and job advantages; it may be a social desirable marriage, or a convinced Christian way of life.

Whatever our goal for our children may be, we cannot help communicating it to them and this is proper enough when kept within reasonable limits. But our ambitions are not easily controlled and the pressure we do not mean to apply adds to the more obvious pressures of study, exams, the new job or the love affair. 'Have you done your homework? You'll never be a doctor if you don't', may sound a harmless enough spur on to the inevitable drudgery, but in fact it amounts to dangerous psychological blackmail.

The normal teenager tries very hard to live up to his parents' expectations, though he may not do it as obviously as he did years before when his play aped almost everything Dad did. The obvious signs disappear at adolescence, but the identification with parents remains, running deep below the surface and influencing the teenager's behaviour strongly. When he fails to live up to what he knows they expect, it affects him deeply. Guilt, disappointment and frustration make a hard dose of mixture to swallow and it is not surprising that he is often touchy. So is his sister for exactly similar reasons.

The effort to live up to his parents does put the teenager under pressure, but it also helps to give stability and a sense of direction during the earlier teen years. This will be helpful, providing the teenager gradually replaces his parents' aspirations with his own. This does not necessarily happen easily. Yet sometime Bob has to stop following in his father's steps and start making his own; June has to grow out of being 'our daughter'. They have to become themselves – adults in their own right, rather than *our* children. This is exactly what adolescence is about.

Strangely enough, it is the teenager who has

remained very stable and who has 'given his parents no trouble' during adolescence who often ends up having and being the biggest problem. He has 'been no trouble to his parents', probably because he accepted their views and their aspirations for longer than most other teenagers. His friends began to find themselves earlier and their parents found them in varying degrees 'troublesome'. Our less troublesome teenager carries on unperturbed right to the end of secondary school before a combination of circumstances forces a change. Decisions about his future career now have to be made; exam pressures find out his lack of personal inner drive. His parents' second-hand will for his success is inadequate now and he lacks a conviction of his own. He is brought up short by an identity crisis – who is he, himself or his parents' child?

In extreme cases this identity crisis can lead to mental breakdown, though this is rare. For the majority there is a sharp readjustment which may involve a change of job or college course, a move out of home to a flat, or something of the kind. If this happens to you with your older teenager, recognise the symptoms and accept that it will probably be for the best. Certainly you cannot achieve anything by continuing to try to stamp your nearly adult child into the mould you had in mind. Possibly you have tried to do so for too long already, or possibly this is just the natural point where in your family situation he needs to go it alone.

So undue pressure has unfortunate consequences. The other extreme is bad too. The home that gives children no incentive or encouragement often results in rather spineless products who achieve little in life. Here is one way in which parents need a delicate touch, avoiding pressure and yet providing the stimulus, motivation and practical help our teenage children need.

Even when we succeed in holding this balance, it isn't easy to help our teenagers map out their future in this complex modern world. There are so many possible openings and all the time careers are getting more specialised and entrance requirements more detailed. Careers advice is now such a specialised field that most of us feel hopelessly lost and opt out altogether. We appear not to care, which is damaging, when the real explanation is that we are lost ourselves.

Alternatively our ignorance makes us fuss, which gets everybody uptight about the future. Uninformed caring inevitably produces tension and resistance. A teenager, facing the bewildering variety of the modern technological job scene, feels as though he is at the entrance of a maze. Without adequate information he's in the dark as well, and when his parents try to push him he does what anyone would do, he refuses to be pushed into a path he can't even see that's leading nowhere very obvious. What he needs in the situation is not more push but more light, more information to enable him to find his way.

Your reaction may be, 'Sure, he's got to have information, but you can't expect me to provide it. I'm as much in the dark as he is'. That may be true, but it doesn't have to be. You can get the information if you try, though that may not be the best thing to do. The real person who needs the information is your teenager and it is usually best to help him find things out for himself, rather than for you to do it for him. You will probably need to advise him on how to go about it, however, and you will need to equip yourself to do this.

Though the vocation and training fields are

complex, there are good advisory services to match and you should make full use of them. The best starting point is probably the school, if your teenager is still at school. There is usually a teacher who keeps files of information about jobs and training of all kinds, and who will also know better than anyone how to go about finding out anything not already on file. The school will also be visited regularly by a professional careers officer who talks to classes and individuals.

You may need to think about how best to make the school approach, especially if the question of jobs and the future is already a pressure point. You don't want to create a position where the teenager is the meat in a home-school sandwich, adding another pressure from the other side. Nor do you want to get him all uptight about the future. It would be better to let him drop out for a year if he can't find the kind of further study that will motivate him.

We faced this with one of ours, who was in a real turmoil as to what to do when he left school. He clearly had the capacity for higher study but had no idea in what direction to head. After hours and hours of talk over much of his final year he had more or less decided to go and get a job, perhaps at the other end of the country, and use the next year to sort himself out before resuming study. Then one day he came home and said, 'Tony Bladon came to school today and told us about what he's doing at college. Sounds just the kind of thing I'd be really interested in.'

And so it turned out. He went to talk to his school careers teacher. Later he got the appropriate handbook from the college. It took a lot of sorting out; we pored over it together for hours till in the end he knew enough to go back to the college and ask the right questions. On those answers he made his decisions, and he's never looked back.

The first step for a teenager at school, then, is to go and see the careers teacher. Things may well flow on naturally and satisfactorily from there. If there is a hang-up, because he doesn't make the approach, or doesn't bring you any feedback, or doesn't seem to get the help he needs, then you could ring up the careers teacher and talk to him.

Before or after leaving school, there is plenty of advice and information to be obtained from careers offices, universities, polytechnics and other colleges. It is, in fact, relatively easy to get the advice your teenager needs. It may be much harder for him to reach a decision and still harder again for you to accept that decision. In fact you may not be very happy about the advice given by the school in the first place. This can be a real source of tension between school and parents, most of whom have high aspirations for their children. While a few older people who left school at 14 or 15 find it hard to see why their children need all this education, most parents aim high for their children rather than low, which is both natural and right.

The biggest difficulties arise when a child seems to have capabilities well below those of his father. The skilled mechanic doesn't like his son being an unskilled labourer and the university lecturer finds it hard to believe that his daughter can't make university. Yet, statistics being what they are, these things often happen. It still doesn't make it easy to accept when it happens to you.

It is nevertheless a fact that the school or other careers officer is in a much better position to assess a student's capability than parents are. Of course it is difficult to accept that your hoped-for little swan is only a rather ordinary goose, but the best way of preventing him being a successful and happy goose is to try and turn him into a swan. If the school adviser suggests a career at a particular level you will be wise to go along with that advice.

Choosing careers and school courses are part of the wider problem of school-parent liaison. Again there is a delicate balance to be achieved, that of good contact without putting a squeeze on the student. Without good contact we only see the school through the eyes of the child and that picture may be a bit distorted. Take the teacher who so constantly picks on your little darling. The whole story sounds so different when you hear first-hand that the darling of your home is the recognised fiend of lower 4B! It will help the teacher of lower 4B too to find that his pet hate has quite reasonable parents, if you manage to keep your cool and be reasonable.

There, of course, comes the crunch. Can you remain calm and reasonable when your child is under fire? We have found it very hard indeed. All the protective instincts with which nature endows parents come rushing into play, our hackles rise and, before we know where we are, lower 4B teacher has problem parents behind his problem pupil. Now he knows exactly why the pupil is such a pain in the neck. Just look at his parents!

Homework is another problem area. How much help should parents give? If they can, that is! Here the teacher's normal practice provides the model. He rarely does the whole problem and certainly not a whole assignment for a student. He looks for the bottle-neck, explains what isn't understood, gives an example and sends the student off to try on his own.

52

Modern educational trends are rightly away from the regular three-hour grind each night. But that makes it difficult for parents to know when required work is not being done. Then, suddenly, a bad report brings it all to light. Again school contact will help, but watch the meat-in-the-sandwich problem.

As we are writing this book we can see families all round us who illustrate what this chapter is trying to say. Our own family illustrates it too, though we have not had an extreme identity crisis to cope with yet. We know a girl whose parents probably have, unintentionally, pressed her far too hard. Since she was very young they have talked a medical career at her. Now she has had to leave school without taking her 'A' levels and take a job for a few months to sort herself out. If her parents are to blame, their daughter does not show any resentment and their real understanding in the present situation makes the prospects for their future relationship bright. In the meantime she has to find her way through a fairly intense identity crisis.

Then we see the young man who has had to pull out of his architecture studies. Looking back on it, he was probably a sitting duck for an identity crisis. He was rather immature at school and certainly no trouble. He respected his parents and accepted their plans for him without qualms and during the school years their communication was reasonable if not wonderful. Conscientiously ploughing through the school course he achieved results well above those his school expected of him. But college studies and adult student life found him out. He didn't really feel he wanted to be an architect, but he didn't know what else to do. He dropped out of his studies but even that he did most tentatively, fiddling around at home for weeks before finding himself a job. He will take time to find himself, but he is essentially a sound young man, so we have no doubt that he will do so.

These are two of the less fortunate ones, two of the minority who strike some degree of serious difficulty. It would be unbalanced not to include a word picture of one of the many luckier youngsters among our friends. Max is fortunate indeed and we wonder how we would have measured up had we been his parents. It appeared early in his schooling that he had abnormal difficulty with reading. In spite of a period of special schooling it soon became clear that he could not hope to complete a full secondary school course. This was a great disappointment to his parents whose elder children had done quite well, but they faced the situation squarely and, outwardly at least, with commendable lack of fuss. They gave Max every possible help and encouragement but managed to avoid any of the underlying pressure.

After three years Max left school to become an apprentice tradesman. His parents had made the openings for him to examine a number of trades carefully, leaving him to choose which ones to explore for definite openings. Max looked the possibilities over and for good if earthy reasons chose most suitably and is doing very well. He knows he is going to find it hard to give his children the standard of living he has so far enjoyed himself, but his approach is most positive. He will have to end up running his own business, not just working for wages. He knows it because he has worked it out for himself, not because his parents have instilled the idea into him. Best of all, he lives at home in a most satisfactory relationship with his parents.

Yes, of course, as parents we have ambitions for our

children. It is natural that we should have and it may be helpful too, provided we discipline those ambitions. We must discipline them particularly when we face the situation that one of our children cannot achieve what we have hoped for. We must be equally disciplined when we have an older teenager who just cannot decide what to do. Pushing him into something just to see him settled is unlikely to work out well in the long run. The parents' function in this very trying situation is first to act as a sounding board for his ideas. We may need to offer suggestions and to make openings for the teenager to investigate for himself. Do not get unduly distressed if the first course of action leads into a blind alley. Your child will be in good company in making an about turn and starting again!

9 *Social life . . . and control?*

A few years ago writers used to warn parents about the serious dangers of being too strict. Discipline was inhibiting; it repressed the child's personality; it left psychological scars! Children needed to express themselves, or they would rebel and become a problem to everyone. A lot of children were allowed to grow up with virtually no control and become, inevitably . . . little horrors!

We have learnt a lot since those days. It is now clear to most people that while over-strict, especially unsympathetic, control does produce a violent kick-back, the damage done by too little control is just as serious, though different. Here again parents need to find a rather delicate balance; they have to exercise firm control, but to do so with real understanding.

The word 'control' can have various shades of meaning. It can convey total domination, something rightly abhorrent to the teenager of today. The control which parents exercise over their teenage children should be something very different, a general framework for behaviour and action, outside which the teenager knows absolutely clearly it is no use trying to go. In this sense control and discipline are closely related. They are at their very best when those subject to them are completely unconscious of them.

We recall a boys' camp in which we were involved

some years ago, a rather difficult camp at which a small uncooperative group had made it necessary to exercise firmer control than we normally wished to impose in a holiday camp. The pay-off came when the mother of one of those uncooperative boys told us some time later that her son's comment on the camp had been, 'It was fabulous, mum, there was absolutely no discipline!' We felt one of those rare moments of real success!

The best control, then, is that of which the controlled are unconscious, and the home is ideally set up to produce it. To begin with, our children know only our home atmosphere and the standards of behaviour we practise. By the time school introduces outside influences, the child knows quite clearly what is expected and what is not tolerated in the home. This all happens unconsciously; the home is transmitting its own value system, which will usually be a strong permanent influence on its products. They will only be rebelled against if the home's requirements have been extreme and unsympathetically enforced.

This general framework of control carries through from childhood to adolescence. Within it the young child is supervised in detail, he is made to clean his teeth, tidy his room, do his homework and so on; but all this has to give way progressively to the self-control of the maturing individual. The word 'progressively' is the important one. One hears occasionally of children brought up with virtually no freedom of choice at all, until suddenly on their 18th or 21st birthday or on getting a first job they are given the key of the door and, without any preparation, sudden freedom to do whatever they wish. The result is, usually, disaster!

Some of the most ticklish questions of control

concern our children's social lives. Where should a 14-year-old be allowed to go alone? What time should a 15-year-old be required home? Or a 17-year-old? Parents who are looking for nice cut-and-dried answers to these questions may find this book disappointing. We doubt whether there are cut-and-dried answers, even within our own family. The children are all so different, the circumstances of various social activities vary so much. Other families must be different again.

Clearly, parents of 13-year-olds must decide what their children will do and where they will go, but there must be sufficient progress over the next five years to ensure that at 18 the former child responsibly makes the right decisions without reference to us. While the older teenager or young adult is living at home, common courtesy suggests that he will tell his parents where he is going, but this must not be taken as asking permission.

A practical point here in regard to the 'all the others are going, mum' line, which all parents come across sooner or later. In fact, what others of the same age are actually doing is a helpful guide to what we may consider reasonable. However, our children do not always distinguish clearly (at least to us) between what the others really are doing and what they would like to be doing. A quiet off-the-record check with one or two other parents may be a help here, though be sure to keep it off the record.

We remember an occasion when after-the-school-dance parties were all the rage. Everyone was going and it was going to be in the captain of the school's home, so it must be all right. As a prefect, our son just had to be there; it really was his duty as a prefect. That was how he saw it. We did not really like it, but were we going to be the only 'square' parents? One phone-call to a close friend revealed another very uneasy parent, who offered to ring the mother of the captain of the school.

'Well', replied Mrs Captain of the School, 'I had heard there was to be some little get-together. At my place? Certainly not, that hasn't even been mentioned. Thank you for letting me know what's in mind.'

A week later a casual conversation at home:

'Oh, that after-dance party . . . '

'Eh?'

'That after-the-dance party.'

'Yes?'

'Don't you want to go now?'

'We've decided not to have it.'

'Oh, I see.'

The story could be taken wrongly. It is not meant to advocate double dealing, or pulling strings behind the scenes. Any blatant or frequent interference will certainly become obvious and be deeply resented. But that wasn't what we set out to do; we were just trying to find out how other parents were handling a situation in which our children were involved together.

We need to remember that in these years there are many social pressures with which our children are not yet fully equipped to cope. They need our help, even though they may not ask for it in so many words. On one occasion our daughter, aged 16, showed us an invitation to a party and asked if she could go. On making inquiries from the mother of the girl giving the party and other mothers we were not reassured! On telling our daughter we would rather she did not go, we were somewhat surprised when she replied, 'Oh good, I was hoping you would say that!' She too had felt uneasy but just needed that moral support to help her say no.

Home parties for young people have caught many parents in a highly successful teenage confidence trick. Comments like 'You're too square, Dad, the kids wouldn't like you being there!' have given parents such an inferiority complex in the face of the younger generation that they feel they have to hide in an obscure corner of their own home and avoid being seen. Meanwhile the young fry make whoopee all over the house. Some parents take the line of least resistance and go out for the evening. Then they wonder why the party got out of hand.

One thing is absolutely certain. If the party is held in our home, then we should be there, and if our children go to a party in someone else's home it is only common sense to make sure that the parents will be home. The question arises, though, as to what 'being home' means. If it does not mean keeping out of the way, it does not have to mean running the show either. Young people like to run their own functions in their own way, casual though it may seem to us, and they usually handle the job pretty well. Why not leave them to do it? Meanwhile, we, as parents, can quietly go ahead with what we would be doing anyway. Mum may need, or want, to help in the kitchen. Our own experience is that we can just 'be around' quite naturally and have an opportunity to get to know our children's friends without being a damper in any way and certainly without obviously supervising.

When the children go out to an evening function one of the obvious things to do is to ensure that they come home within a reasonably short time of the end of the function. A definite time-to-be-home-by helps

60

teenagers to know where they stand. They can nearly always ring up if they are delayed and should be taught to consider our feelings in this way.

The motor car is still a growing source of trouble and tragedy among youth today. Many accidents are caused by young adults who are beyond parental control but there are others for which parents must accept at least part of the blame. The wealthy parent who gives a teenager a car for passing his 'A' levels may be putting a lethal weapon into hands too irresponsible to control it properly. It is just as well that most families cannot afford to do this, but the average parent may have to control the use of the family car firmly on some occasions.

The question of control inevitably raises that of punishment, something which is often necessary in some form for younger children. It may, on occasions, be necessary to punish the mid-teenager, though we need to be very sure that the punishment is really needed by the teenager. Sometimes the real need for punishment seems to spring from our injured parental pride and from our desire to reassert ourselves. Looking back on our own family we did not often punish our teenagers, and probably we needed to punish them even less than we actually did. Let us hasten to add – this was not because they were angels!

The fact is that teenagers' strongly developed sense of guilt punishes them for us when they fail. Without rubbing in our concern or displeasure it will be obvious enough, and this automatically increases the sense of failure. A serious breach of trust inevitably brings in its train the temporary withdrawal of our trust. Taking away some privileges may need to be added in an extreme case, but not hastily or frequently. The best form of punishment, if it can be called such, is to allow teenagers to take the consequences of their unacceptable behaviour, suffering any embarrassment or inconvenience which results.

Obviously there are limits to the lengths to which it is possible to carry this policy. We can let a 16-year-old suffer the possible consequences of having an untidy room, or of being absent from an important social function to which duty calls him. We obviously could not responsibly allow him to risk the consequences of a drug party or of entering a car with an alcohol-affected driver. In between these extremes lies a whole spectrum of possible situations. How far should we impose control? To what extent should we protect our children?

Clearly some parents do over-protect their children and produce rather spineless dependent individuals as a result. A few go to the other extreme so that their children collapse under the strain of challenges which are quite beyond their capabilities. Here perhaps is the guideline. We should let our teenage children face any situation they have a reasonable prospect of handling. Successfully meeting a demanding challenge is the most maturing experience possible, but of course any real challenge involves the possibility of failure. Holiday jobs and expeditions with friends are excellent chances for teenagers to learn by experience. Mistakes cost little because nothing permanent is involved.

There is a danger that we, as parents, will decide what our children are capable of handling and only let them face what we think will be good for them. This is nearly always a mistake. It is far better to let them decide for themselves what they are ready to face and to stand behind them in case failure comes along. We may then help to make that failure a maturing rather than a damaging experience.

We can illustrate this well. One of our boys was asked, absolutely unexpectedly, to be house captain at his school. It was a great honour and a greater surprise. He had hardly toed the line the year before and he disapproved of the rigid line taken by the school establishment. He asked us what we thought he should do. It was a hard question to answer in any case. On the one hand we wanted him to have the valuable experience of such responsibility. On the other hand we wanted to protect him from the divided loyalties we knew would take a toll of his sensitive nature. But of course both reactions were centred on what *we* wanted. We are glad that, having pointed out both sides to him, we left the decision to him. He accepted and we all suffered, but he did a first-class job!

Then again we have to realise that, even in one family, the children are different. The same son went and found himself a most suitable holiday job without any prompting, while our daughter needed our help to get her first job. The rule perhaps is this: give the minimum help necessary to get them off the ground. Don't keep on pushing, however uncertain they look to be. If teenagers baulk at difficulties, the important thing is to lead or help them over their problems and to avoid the temptation to prod or ridicule them into action.

The test comes to parents when an older teenager, after due deliberation, seems to arrive at an ill-advised decision. What should we do? There can be only one answer: accept it gracefully. Do not go on expressing disapproval; in fact, even support the teenager to meet the consequences of the decision. Above all resist the temptation to say, 'I told you so'. That will only make the teenager more determined to stick to the decision when he knows deep down that he should go back on it.

The best protection that any parents can give their children is unquestionably the ability to make their own decisions responsibly. We are aiming to help them learn to discriminate, and anything that hinders this will in the long run hinder them.

10 *Looking in the mirror*

Discriminate . . . between right and wrong; between a good party to go to and one that may be better left alone; between a good friend and a bad one. These are some of the powers of discrimination we want to see our teenagers develop.

There is another form of discrimination they also develop, whether we like it or not, and sometimes we won't. They apply their growing powers of discrimination to us, their parents. They look at our actions and they listen to our words, and they are puzzled. The two don't match up. So they have to discriminate. Which one will they be influenced by, our actions or our words?

What you really are

So our children's adolescence brings us to the crunch. Actions always speak louder than words; what we are is always more real than what we say. Now what we really are has caught up with us. Gone are the days when we could say 'Do what I tell you' and be sure of being obeyed. 'But *you* don't do it', or 'why shouldn't I, if you can?' is thrown back at our unreasonable order.

Suddenly the smoker finds himself hunting for reasons why his son shouldn't smoke too, the heavy drinker thanks his stars for the minimum drinking age, and the non-church-going couple find Sunday School days are over. The adolescent is learning to discriminate and he, quite rightly, wants reasons why he should behave or act in some particular way. 'Because I say so' never was a good reason, but now it just won't do at all. And watch it if it seems to work.

The teenager may not smoke openly at home if he's been forbidden to, but he will almost certainly try it out elsewhere. He may not be able to drink beer because his parents won't let him and he looks too young to buy it, but the glass of beer remains a symbol of that elusive adult status he's trying to reach.

It isn't only our aspirations for our children that are transmitted unconsciously to them. For example, all four of ours are voracious readers, but then we both love reading and the house is full of books. We never made our children read; we didn't have to, they just caught the habit. Our eldest two both married the products of non-reading homes and their partners, though well educated, read little.

The same thing applies to every aspect of life. The home passes on a whole life-style, in all its complexity. In later chapters we'll look at this specifically in relation to sex and religion. But, in fact, it covers the whole of life and especially the general scale of values on which our teenagers are going to make their moral decisions. They will get that scale mainly from us, though other influences will modify the details.

There is no smokescreen to hide behind, either. It is not what we pretend to be that really influences our children. Their discrimination may be partly unconscious, but it is remarkably acute. They see us as we really are, not as we would like to appear, and that is why we have to turn the mirror on ourselves.

Basic values

The flux of modern society makes basic values much more important than they would be in a stable society. How many of us have quailed at the responsibility of fitting a 12-year-old to cope with adult life in six years' time. What will society be like then? What will be the challenges he'll have to face? What new pitfalls will have to be avoided? None of us can see clearly even six years ahead any more. How on earth can we prepare him for the unknown?

This is where we have found the absolutes of Jesus' teaching a great help. The world may change, circumstances alter beyond recognition, society turn itself inside out, but the basic values governing human relationships stay the same. The humanist agrees broadly with the Christian on that, however much he differs on the basis from which he derives those values. It is by giving our teenagers sound values that we equip them for the unknown future.

That makes a parent think, doesn't it? The two of us have had to stop from time to time and ask how our children were seeing our life-style. There was a patch when, in retrospect, material things were beginning to mean too much to us. Three years in New Guinea fixed that and we are thankful. It would be hard to name particular things we did differently, but our basic outlook was changed and that change came through to our children.

Having teenage children really puts the quality of our own lives under the searchlight, we find. Today people are very concerned about the social and environmental quality of life, but what about the moral quality of our lives? That reflects our values much more directly. We all want our children to be honest and truthful, but do we provide them with a model? Or do we tell them to tell that inconvenient caller that we are out when we are in? Are we appalled if they cheat in exams, when we boast of what we have got past the income tax man?

Surely there is no need to go on. The point is obvious enough. What we *are* is what really counts. Speaking personally, we can only share how much being Christians has meant to us. At the heart of Christianity is a message of power, God's power to live life as He wants us to, and what we have discovered to be a reality. We would not like to have brought up teenagers without this.

Your social life

In the last chapter we talked about teenagers' social life. Obviously the social life of us the parents will have its influence on theirs. They won't model their social activities on ours – rather the reverse – but the motives behind will be powerful. The socialite mum, who isn't interested in other people but is quite happy to use them to get places, will often produce a daughter who regards social life the same way. The family who measure the success of a party in gallons of beer give their children a model for their future adult lives.

Friends and relatives

Friends and relatives can be quite a problem too, especially if your values are pretty different from theirs. Our children have always got on well with the families of our friends and through school they have made many friends from homes very different from ours. They have gone to stay in them, quite often, and at times we have been a bit concerned. Would they, for example, be harmed by television programmes we didn't watch, by language we tried to avoid? Would they get the idea that Sunday is the day for the beach rather than church? Would they . . . ? The fears could be endless.

The extent to which this is your problem will depend so much on your set-up. You may have little contact with close relatives or you may have a lot. Your children may have lots of opportunities to go away on their own or they may have very few. What being under the influence of other life-styles does is to test your children's personal value system. We have preferred our children to undergo these tests in small doses, throughout their teenage years, rather than sheltering them altogether till they suddenly face the great exam of being out in the adult world on their own.

The teenager with sound values will look at what others do, use his powers of discrimination and reach his own conclusions. Friends and relatives are unlikely to cause a sudden change in his value system. They may exert a gradual influence, and they may affect behaviour in a way that will require wisdom, patience and discrimination from parents. If your 13-year-old son comes home from a week with a friend swearing like a trooper you will have to take corrective action. If your 17-year-old daughter comes home from a week away with her nature-fresh face plastered with make-up you may be wise to say nothing. In between it may be hard to know whether to say or do anything and, if so, what.

The real thing, though, is that neither of these examples nor many other possibilities represent a real change in values. The swearing was just a bad habit picked up, the make-up an experiment. What we of the older generation find so difficult is to distinguish between the values we hold and the modes of behaviour by which we express those values. We assume that people who act differently must have different values, presumably worse ones. We demand that our children express the values of our home in exactly the same way as we do, when they could work out quite different behaviour patterns without throwing any of our basic values away.

So sound values are a vital thing to pass on to our children and our whole life-style, conscious and unconscious, is the transmitter. Failure to provide sound values may be a serious thing. It is the teenager who lacks an adequate value system of his own who will be easily influenced by the people he is with. He may be quite deeply influenced by short periods with friends or relatives.

Once again we come back to the mirror. There is no *certain* way of putting our teenagers on the right road for life, but we've got a much better chance of doing so if we know the road ourselves. Let us each take a hard, long look at the way we live.

Sex lies right at the heart of the changes which are occurring during adolescence. That is obvious enough but somehow . . . well, if only it didn't! Bringing up children is difficult enough without that complication!

Once again the parents' underlying approach is the key to the situation. If we have hang-ups about sex ourselves it is inevitable that we shall pass them on to our children. On the other hand, if we are quite relaxed about the subject our children will inherit from us the important gift of regarding sex quite naturally. It should be a privilege to point our children towards a sound attitude about sex and to the likelihood of a satisfying sexual life of their own.

Somehow this is not easy for many parents. We realise that sexual drives are going to be important during our teenagers' sexual maturing and that their desire for mixed company is entirely natural. We know we should be thankful that they are being entirely normal in finding the opposite sex interesting. After all, we do! Yet it is hard to be completely at ease about this development in our children. There is so much involved; such important things are at stake and there are such frightening possibilities if things go wrong.

Of course, in one sense our worst fears are justified. We have lived long enough to see the ghastly unhappiness which sex misused can bring about. We want, at all costs, to protect our children from this kind of thing. That is commendable enough. But how are we going to do it? Certainly not by trying to hold the lid on a highly explosive box, by failing to face squarely and openly that sex is soon going to have the same adult place in our children's lives that it has in our own. How then?

Children need two main things from their parents in the field of sex. They need adequate accurate information, and they need a sound outlook and approach – a sound philosophy of sex if you like. The outlook is of course the more important of the two, and this is where some sex education programmes fail. They seem to imply that as long as children are informed about sex that is all that is necessary. However, it is also true that without information as a basis no sound outlook is possible. Information is essential.

Information? 'He probably knows more than I do' may be your first reaction. This may be true in individual cases, but it would be a very unwise parent who acted on such an assumption. There is plenty of reliable evidence that ignorance about the facts of sex remains a major problem for a lot of young people. Certainly school biology courses do a lot, 'human relations' is commonly included in the school programme these days, youth groups show films and so on; but we still need to ensure that each of our children is equipped with the basic information about sex.

Ideally this programme of informing should be well on the way before adolescence. A survey entitled *The facts of life for children* in *Crusade*, May 1972, recommended for the 9-13 age group, among others, *Where do babies come from?* by Jill Kenner (National Marriage Guidance Council), *Almost Twelve* by Kenneth

Taylor (Coverdale House Publishers), and *The Facts of Life for Children* by Roger Pilkington (available from Family Doctor, 47-51 Chalton Street, Euston, London, NW1). You may know of other things. However, the way in which information is given is almost as important. It will convey to the child what outlook on sex the parents have. The father who rather shamefacedly slips his son a book with a somewhat awkward 'you may find this interesting' conveys unmistakably a view that sex is embarrassing and rather shameful. The parents who have learnt how to talk about these things naturally are giving their children, in the most desirable way, the outlook that sex is a normal, natural part of life.

Free discussion of sex is a most important element in parent-child communication; it seems to make the relationship deeper than it would otherwise be. Of course it can lead to those embarrassing moments when grandma is horribly shocked. This can be awkward, but it is hardly disastrous, and the children quickly come to appreciate the kind of things it is better to avoid discussing while grandma is present! We have occasionally received a jolt ourselves at the sauciness of a joke that our children have felt free to share with us, but a good laugh about a genuinely funny story with a sexual theme is one of the very best ways of removing that special forbidden aura from the topic.

Some parents are rather afraid of the permissive attitudes to sex which are influencing their children today. Now, it is quite certain that the attitudes of young people today are permissive sexually, as well as in other respects. In the survey previously referred to, only 25% of the male teenagers and 53% of the female ones said they regarded sexual relations as being for

73

marriage only, while 50% of the boys and 14% of the girls opted for the two answers which expressed the view that sexual relations were permissible without any settled relationship of love or approaching marriage. These views were widely spread through the community. Country children were a little more conservative, as were those actively connected with churches, though not nearly as much so as some clergy would have wished. In fact one minister was so shocked by the responses of his church young people to this question that he refused to forward us the entire set of questionnaires for processing!

So young people, our teenage children, do have a relatively permissive attitude to sex. They are reluctant to judge others to be wrong in what they are doing. It is also true that attitudes quite strongly influence actions. But. in the realm of sex particularly, there may be a very wide gap between what we accept as normal behaviour for people in general, and what we will actually do ourselves. To begin with, the more conservative attitude of girls (for obvious reasons) limits the opportunity of the young male to translate his permissive outlook into practice. Youthful attitudes also contain an element of bravado, which might well not survive even if a favourable opportunity did present itself. And so far as opportunity is concerned, surely this is where we as parents have the prime responsibility to see that our children meet the opposite sex under circumstances which naturally restrict the scope for sexual adventure.

There is well-supported evidence from research that youthful action is much more conservative than youth's sexual attitudes. Some popular writers and speakers seem to suggest that the majority of young people are sexually promiscuous. Not one published survey supports this view. Only a relatively small proportion of young people go to the length of full sexual intercourse. A university survey suggests that only a small proportion of these is truly promiscuous; the majority are involved in a steady relationship which may or may not lead to marriage.

Those of us who have strong Christian views, or are deeply imbued with what some people like to label 'middle-class morality', may deplore that the situation is as far from our ideal as it is. But those are the facts and we need to face them – seeing the situation neither as worse than it really is, nor as better, but realistically. This is the world for which we have to prepare our children. They will have to make their own choices in the end – about sexual behaviour as about anything else. They will make those decisions on the basis of what we have imparted to them, both consciously and unconsciously.

The unconscious part of sex education is perhaps the more important and it provides, in a real sense, a test of the quality of our marriage. Through the advertising media, the glossy magazines and in many other ways our teenage children have a dangerously false view of sex presented to them. The pleasures of sex are divorced from the basic context of the human relationship of which they form only a part. It is the depersonalisation of sex that is pernicious and which in the extreme case becomes pornography.

When the right moment comes we should point out to our children how dangerous and wrong this is. But the best protection from this false view of sex comes through the atmosphere of a home at the centre of which is a really sound sex relationship. Teenagers from such a background come to realise that the human relationships are important and that a superficial view of sex cheapens the relationship. This unconscious feeling of what the sex relationship is about is the underlying key to future behaviour, though it needs to be supported by specific information and by the informal teaching of family discussion.

Even if we do succeed in transmitting to our children a sound basic attitude to sex and also in equipping them with the necessary factual information, we cannot expect to escape difficulties altogether. Social activities are, in due course, likely to lead to 'pairing off' and, while the general principles of control we have suggested still apply, the degree to which parents can exercise direct control becomes more limited.

The pattern of 'between-sex' relationships changes as our adolescent children develop. Although we cannot draw precise dividing lines, our children will probably go through four recognisable phases, each of which needs to be handled in its own way.

Group mixing

This phase covers the years of puberty proper. These years will vary from child to child from as early as nine to as late as 15 plus. There is a tendency for sexual maturity to come at a much earlier age than was so for us their parents. Interest in the opposite sex is rather a general one. Particular girls (or boys) are, of course, the focus of this interest, but social needs are satisfied by being in mixed company. Not uncommonly the boys stick together, as do the girls, but activities are mixed!

Parents are mainly concerned with two matters: control of the activities, and control of the process of going to and from them, both of which were discussed in chapter 9. While common sense is often sufficient, do not expect things to be plain sailing.

Pairing off

By 'pairing off' we understand one boy going out with one girl without others necessarily being present. The couple may be going somewhere with others, but essentially just one pair is involved. It will almost certainly arise naturally out of the earlier group phase. How early should we allow our children to pair off like this? Perhaps some parents would prefer to ask, 'How long can we hope to stop it?' particularly when one sees invitations addressed to a 13-year-old for 'Joe Bloggs and partner' to attend a birthday party. Interestingly our 13-year-old ignored the partner bit and found that almost all the other boys had done the same. In his circle, at least, 13-year-old boys were not interested in partners.

Certainly by mid-teens, school socials and dances if not 'discos' in town will have involved your 15-year-old in finding a partner. This may have been easily achieved by a small group of three or four boys and girls going together, but equally it could have been embarrassing for the 'odd couple' left who are then forced together. However, modern dancing does not insist on the partnership principle in the same way as 'old time', so there is not the pressure on the young person to have a particular partner. Indeed, young people today will often have a number of boy or girl friends whom they accompany to different activities at this stage.

During the final school years the pressures of work are such that opportunity for social life is limited. This often means that there is only time for one partner and so they slip past the 'pairing off' stage into the going steady phase. The important thing seems to be for parents to accept whatever naturally develops as long as the relationship has no seriously undesirable features. Be sure not to make the teenager who remains unattached feel he is lacking. There is nothing worse than the happily-free 17-year-old being forced to embark on an unwanted friendship 'just to please mum' or to fit in with 'what everybody else is doing'.

Going steady is a natural development of stage 2, and it will normally intensify gradually to **courtship and engagement.**

The last three phases all call for parents to adopt an approach of unobtrusive watchfulness. The difficulty is that watchfulness so easily becomes snooping, while even reasonable supervision may be interpreted as distrust, if real trust has not been developed earlier. If we have given our children sound sexual attitudes, they will usually value our guidance and accept sensible cautions, so long as they are not sounded at the wrong moment.

After all, every human society regulates the circumstances in which young men and women may be alone together. Because this 'regulating' is very loose in our modern society, most of the control now has to come from the 'family society'. It is parents who are left to control the dates and other outings of their teenagers. They may love to talk about whom they saw and what they did on these outings; if not it may be difficult to know where they have been. They can pull the wool over our eyes, but if they do, something will eventually give them away.

The advent of the car rather complicates things; its combination of privacy and mobility opens up so many possibilities. Parked in a secluded spot, it provides today's number one setting for the romantic interlude. It is fortunately out of reach of the younger teenager who lacks car, driving licence and older friends with both. But sooner or later the problem will catch up with your family and you may need to keep the family car suitably employed at times. The real aim, however, must be to have brought your 18-year-old to a point of personal responsibility.

Helping children through the various phases of opposite sex relationships to personal responsibility has an important positive side. Negative supervision to 'keep them out of trouble' is quite insufficient on its own. There has to be positive guidance and encouragement in developing the right kind of friendships too. If we stand behind them sensitively we can help our children to interact confidently with the opposite sex and learn to handle them as real people.

One final word needs to be added. In the intensely personal matter of sex we must aim to be able to trust our children. How nice to hear, 'We couldn't have embarked on pre-marital sex, our parents trusted us too much'. Of course such trust cannot be conjured out of the air. First comes our influence and training, the absorbing of sound standards; then as the teenage years roll by, we get many little signs of what standards our children are adopting. Not only their actions, but comments on their friends, their friends' parents – most revealing – and on the actions of public figures show us what they are thinking. Then gradually we can loosen the reins, and, rather nervously, trust.

It is obviously more difficult to give uninhibited trust where so much is at stake, yet this is what we have to work towards. Our teenagers are growing up under circumstances in which they will certainly be able to find opportunities for sexual adventure if they are determined to do so. The opportunities may even present themselves without being particularly sought. What we have to do is to impart to them sexual attitudes which will make them want to use their freedom responsibly. Only in this way will our teenagers grow into responsible young adults.

12 *Church and all that jazz*

The subject of the last chapter was a very personal one. The field of religion is even more so. To some it is of little importance. Many more feel vaguely puzzled by religion; some wish they could give their children a more definite faith than they themselves have managed to find. To us Christianity has been basic, a vital force in our personal and family lives, and that makes for a difficulty in writing this chapter. To make sure it does not turn into a sermon, it is probably best to write down simply how God has helped us as a family.

In our case we both started out on marriage as convinced Christians. If God were to give us children, we hoped from the start to lead them to the point where they would find Him as vital in their lives as we had done. Our children have not therefore had the kind of shake-up experienced by some young friends of ours. They used to tell us, with humour but deep feeling, of what happened at home when hard-drinking father came home to say, 'Well, that's that. I'm a Christian now!' They could scarcely deny the power of Christ to change lives; they had seen both their parents and the home transformed and were thoroughly convinced. Our children would somehow have to be convinced in less dramatic ways and that, in part, is the problem which faces parents of definite Christian convictions.

Our religious family *activities* had been few, though each one has, in retrospect, been very important. Prayer at bedtime has been a basic one, started before each child was old enough to be more than vaguely aware of what was happening. We feel sure that an element of true serenity can be communicated by the calm committal of ourselves to God for the night. In many outward ways our rather boisterous home life has not been particularly serene. Yet at different times each of our children has brought us up short in the face of some worry by the calm assumption that 'surely God will take care of it, Mummy?'!

Prayer is important in the family and not just at bedtime or at family prayers. Prayer comes very naturally to little children. If they get used to talking to Jesus about relatively little things then they will know better how to handle the bigger problems which will come later. A spontaneous prayer with a child who is frightened, or in a stew about school work, has often been a real help. Moreover this conveys the idea that it is perfectly natural to take everything to God, as of course it should be.

Bible stories naturally formed part of bedtime reading too, especially on Sundays. 'Sunday stories' like Moses, David and Daniel became very popular and were wanted on other days too. This helped to make Sunday a specially good day without divorcing the Bible from the rest of the week.

Our only other organised religious activity at home has been family prayers. We say 'organised', though there can be nothing more disorganised than trying to get four children between one and ten to sit down and listen at the same time. Rounding them up alone would tax the skills of a highly-trained sheep-dog. 'Now put that car down, Christopher, and don't

run it up and down the table.' 'No, Alison, afterwards
what, Michael, you just can't wait . . . well quickly
then!' The toilet visit by four-year-old completed, the
car again garaged, we are finally seated quietly just
in time for one-year-old to blow the most gorgeous
raspberry. Everyone dissolves! Have you ever tried
to bring your own facial muscles back to that state of
control suited to reading a simple Bible passage?
Remarkably hard!

As the children got older the difficulties became
less – except for the rounding-up problem, that is.
However, the daily (more or less) reading after the
evening meal has been really worthwhile. We have
used a variety of books and courses available from
religious bookshops, choosing one suitable for the
average age of the family. For some time now we have
used the *Family Prayers* published by Scripture Union,
which we have found most suitable to our needs, once
the average age of the children reached seven or
eight. We would usually just read the passage and the
comment, answer the question and finish with a
prayer. This used to be the prerogative of father but
now, with a teenage and older family, various members
of the family read, comment and pray for various needs
and people. Five or six minutes would cover it and we
do not drag it, though every now and again one of the
children will stop us with a question of his own.

These rare unheralded discussions have been worth
their weight in gold, revealing problems and often
things the children have learnt elsewhere. Sometimes
their grasp of a thorny issue has astonished us.

'Where on earth did you learn that, Michael?'

'The Scripture Union, of course.'

The reply was given in a tone of contempt for his
parents' slowness. It was as if he was saying, 'Don't

you read your Bible each morning and provide the wherewithal for the other members of the family to do the same? Don't you expect me to learn?' The answer is, of course, that we do, and that is why we encourage them to read the Bible for themselves as well as round the table as a family. However, we do not regard that as a family religious activity; we don't organise it or supervise it. It's just a habit we practise ourselves and encourage the children to take up if they want to.

You may ask whether these activities at home are necessary. If there is a religious atmosphere in the home, will this not be passed on to the children without a lot of actual religious activity? The answer, of course, is – certainly it will. The awareness of God 'somewhere up there' will undoubtedly come across. But is this enough? It is all that many of today's adults have received from their parents, because a general belief in God without any actual religious practice can do no better. We would not have been satisfied to do so little for our children. Faith involves practice, and it is a practising faith we wanted to pass on to them.

Going to church has also been an important part of our family's religious life. It started for the children with Sunday School, where a suitable one was available. While they were young, our children were not the type to sit through adult services quietly, so there was quite a time when the two of us had to take church-going in turns. Then it became possible to include the children in adult church-going or to leave an unwilling one at home. Family services relevant for all ages are held in many churches now, and this can be a tremendous help. We have tried to avoid too much compulsion; after all, in our kind of home the children

84

get rather a basinful. We have run into refusal to go to Sunday School, the reason being usually social rather than religious: a disliked teacher, bad relationships with other children, for example. We have accepted this refusal at the time and let it work itself out. In our case it always did.

How important is direct church involvement for our children? In one way, perhaps, of little importance, but in another way vital because the church provides expression outside the home for the religious teaching of the home, and this helps to save the home atmosphere from unreality. It is most necessary that teenagers be able to check their religious views and experiences with others from different backgrounds and especially with those who do not come from convinced Christian homes. Church activities thus add in an important way to what happens at home, though religious activities at home and church are, after all, only a framework. We know plenty of families who had them all, and more, and yet the children seem to share little of their parents' faith. It is not activities that communicate faith. Faith is caught, not taught.

This is the thing that has, at various times, frightened us. We try to live as active, dedicated Christians, and we don't do it just for show. Our faith really does matter to us. But our children live with us all the time; they see the most intimate details of our lives, when we are totally off guard at home. They see our inconsistencies, our pettinesses, our lack of self-control and our selfishness. How can we hope that they will see us to be sincere but imperfect, rather than as the hypocrites we must sometimes appear?

There is no simple solution to this very difficult problem – at least we do not know one. Sincerity must be part of the answer and so must humility. We have found our children are wonderful at making allowances, as long as we don't try to put one over them. We try to apologise when we need to. Can we expect them to do so if we don't? They seem to realise that while our actions do reflect some of what we are, they do not always do so perfectly. They are always willing to look behind the regretted action, provided it *is* regretted.

The two qualities of flexibility and understanding are as important on the religious side of life as they are elsewhere. But the more definite one's faith, the more convinced one is of the rightness of one's beliefs and views, the more difficult it is to be flexible in dealing with one's children. Perhaps that is why many convinced Christians find it hard to be flexible. Their inflexibility leads to lack of understanding, which in turn prevents communication.

Then again it has to be faced that the church as a whole has become a most conservative institution, often so conservative that it is really quite out of touch with the world as it now is. It is, we find, not difficult to interest young people in Christianity, but it is often very difficult to get them involved with the church, of which they have a very low opinion. Yet association with a church is important. Our home neither can be nor should be the sole influence on our children. They will be subject to many influences outside the home, in all spheres, not just the religious one. Some of these influences will be good and some will be bad. The personal influence of vital Christian leaders provides a stepping stone from dependence on us as parents to the personal independence of the adult.

It would be side-stepping an important question if we did not include some comments here about the teenager who rebels against his Christian home. This rebellion most commonly shows up in a refusal to attend church or Sunday School, or to participate in some other religious activity. As parents we are embarrassed for fear of what others in the church may be thinking and commonly resort to compulsion. 'You are going to come to church whether you like it or not, at least till . . . ' and we name some time ahead, by when we hope the difficulty will have subsided.

This approach usually fails because it is dealing with the symptom we can see rather than with the cause. The real rebellion is in the underlying attitude, the unwillingness on the part of our children to accept our religious principles and assumptions. There may be many reasons for their unwillingness, none of which will be overcome by compulsion. By its very nature the religious outlook of a person is his own; he may be forced into religious observances, but he cannot be forced into an attitude of mind. Compulsion is simply impossible.

Furthermore, compulsion nearly always creates resentment. It makes us dig our toes in; it makes minor issues into major confrontations and in the end it can make the teenager do exactly the opposite of what his parents want. The serious thing from a Christian point of view is not so much that the teenager often severs connection with the church as an institution, but that he may react altogether against the faith which could enrich his life.

How then is this kind of rebellion to be handled? The first answer must be, calmly and without emotion. Do not read more into the protest about Bible Class than is really there. It may be simply that the class leader is dull, or that your teenager is handling relationships there badly, or that he has grown out of what the group is providing. A few inquiries from those concerned at the church will soon find out whether this is all that is wrong. If it is a change to a different group within the church may solve the problem.

The difficulty may, of course, lie much deeper. Your teenager may be questioning the truth of what you or the church are teaching, and this may be both good and necessary. Rethinking is, in fact, an essential part of the personal shake-up which a teenager needs if he is to replace a parent-supplied second-hand faith by his own personal conviction. Sympathetic understanding can help to guide the shake-up in the direction of the parents' faith; coercion will almost certainly achieve the opposite.

As Christian parents we must be ready to face the possible disappointment that, however wise and understanding we have been, one of our children will forsake the faith in which we have taken such trouble to rear them. When this happens it is easy to blame ourselves or past circumstances for what has happened. No doubt we will have contributed our share to the present situation and a sane recognition of the mistakes we have made may help us to be better parents to our other children. But morbid introspection will help little. We have a present situation to face. What shall we do about it?

Surely Christian principles of action are clear enough. Our love for others should not depend on their agreement with us. We are called to love people none the less and seek as much as ever to preserve our relationship with them, though that relationship will now lack a most important element which we previously had in common. Inevitably this will modify our relationship with our children too, but it need not make it any less sincere or warm. Our children in the end have to make their own choices and have to answer for them to God as well as to society.

Before concluding this chapter we would like to add a word to parents in a rather different position. We meet quite a number who are not convinced Christians themselves, not even regular church attenders, yet they would like to equip their children with a better understanding, a stronger faith than they themselves had. If you are in this group, you just have to recognise that in the long run the most powerful influence on your children will be what you actually are. The best way to lead your children to a faith is to find that faith for yourself. It is not within the scope of this book to go on to describe how you may do this. Obviously a convinced Christian whom you know and respect will be one of the most fruitful sources of help. The New Testament contains one book which the author says he wrote especially to lead people to faith. This is St John's gospel,[1] and reading it carefully in a modern translation is certainly one way to start looking for faith. Remember Christ's promise that he who seeks will find. Faith eludes many of us mainly because we do not look for it.

[1] Scripture Union publish a most helpful booklet of notes on St John's gospel under the title *Invitation to Live*.

13 *Tension – or fun*

So, having teenage children is a serious business and nothing we have written is meant to suggest otherwise. Though serious it can still be fun, providing we relax enough to enjoy it. Our teenage children will reflect our mood, whether it is relaxed or tense. It is we, the parents, who have to keep tension out of the home. We have to resist the temptation to hammer at pressure points, even when we are worked up. Long male hair, unsuitable dress or make-up, loud music we dislike, irresponsibility over study, money, social or religious duty; all these and others may irritate or worry us. It very rarely pays to let fly.

Yet what is the alternative? Can we allow our children to be thoroughly slovenly, inconsiderate and irresponsible? Of course we cannot. The question is not whether we try to influence them or not; it is a question of *how* we try to influence them. In the long run our influence will be more effective and much more lasting if we can exert it without creating tension. Remember the old adage of counting twenty before speaking; speak out by all means, but at the right time and in the right way and tension will be avoided.

You will relax more easily if you really appreciate your children's growing independence. Arguments can be welcomed, personal decisions respected and even the social bricks your teenager drops are more tolerable when seen as part of his growing independence. Want your teenager to try his wings; nothing will make him more tense than the feeling that Mum and Dad just don't want him to grow up. He may get this feeling in various ways. Overprotection, 'good old-fashioned discipline', undue restriction on social life, and above all a general sense of being distrusted make it impossible for teenagers to be relaxed in their relations with their parents. So relax and let them grow up. You will avoid a lot of tension.

Avoiding tension is the negative side of relaxed parenthood. On the positive side there are four key things we have to give our teenagers.

The first is **understanding.** Understanding involves both knowledge about our teenagers and a right attitude to them. Our early chapters have tried to provide some of the necessary knowledge, the whole book seeks to convey what we believe to be the right attitude. We hope it has done so.

Secondly, we must give our teenagers our **trust.** A sense of being trusted quickly develops a sense of responsibility and helps our teenagers to make right decisions for themselves.

The final two are closely linked. We need to give them **ourselves** and this includes particularly our **time.** There is no substitute for our time, and we make a terrible mistake if we think that money or presents can replace it. But in what way do we give ourselves? Obviously we give ourselves to our teenagers emotionally by being involved with them. But we have to make a conscious effort to open up our personalities to them. Most of us draw a blind over our real selves for fear of what others may see there. In modern society this reserve is a big obstacle to communication, an obstacle we should try and keep out of our homes.

It is by knowing us as we really are that our children will get the most help from us. Christian parents may be particularly reserved, for fear that our failures reflect on our professed faith, as well as on ourselves. But the reason is not a valid one. If our children are to learn to share our faith, it must be a real faith. They need to see our struggles and our failures as well as our strengths and successes. Of course, they will see them anyway, but they need to see that we acknowledge them and know how we handle them. Only so will they feel that our faith may be worth trying out in their own lives.

Finally we must all remember that our homes can only be the base from which our children will launch out to make their own lives. We hear too much of the 'sad day when Judy married and left such a gap in our home'. What is sad about that? The sadness seems to reflect a selfishness on the part of parents, a selfishness like that which earlier caused resentment of the influence of others on their children. When our children are adult we should be glad that they have found their own niche and the partner to share it with. Our relationship with them will go on developing new and enjoyable facets now. It is adult life we have been preparing them for. Now they are adult they can offer us a mature relationship which will enrich the remainder of our lives.

Pop in the seventies
Graham Cray

'The man on the radio won't leave me alone . . . ' says a
recent song, and it could speak for a generation. If you
are young, Pop music is inescapable; whether at con-
certs or discos, on radio or TV, as background music in
shops or before football matches, or through magazines
or posters on classroom walls, the voice of Pop cannot be
silenced.

This fact has two main implications for Christian
parents:
1) It is not physically possible, even if it were desirable,
to shield children totally from Pop. Parents who try
usually alienate their children from their own generation
or from themselves.
2) The children of Christian families must be brought up
to discern between the good, the neutral and the harmful
in Pop, even if the parents themselves have little understanding or sympathy with the music.

It is at this stage that a common error is made. Most
adults analyse not Pop *music* but Pop *lyrics*; probably
because, if they can hear them, they are the one part of a
song they can understand. Now clearly lyrics are important; when John Lennon sings, 'God is a concept by
which we measure our pain . . . I don't believe in Bible
. . . I don't believe in Jesus . . . I just believe in me,' he
makes his position plain; but it is only a tiny percentage
of Pop songs which have any sort of message, **and in all
Pop music lyrics are secondary.** Pop is **music of
feeling,** speaking primarily to the body and emotions
and only secondarily to the intellect. Mick Farren has

written, 'Our parents have never really understood Rock 'n' Roll . . . because Rock is not something you understand, it is something that you *feel with your body*, and you know.' In a TV interview the Soul singer Stevie Wonder said, 'Soul is the ability to express what you *feel inwardly* in singing . . . to bring it out where other people can relate to *the feelings you give off*.' Thus you either relate to a piece of Pop music or you don't, and only if you do are you liable to be influenced by its verbal message. Communication from a Pop song is not like communication from a book.

To many Christians this is deeply disturbing, because it means that a message or song can gain acceptance without any real critical analysis of what it says. Indeed the same can be said of TV, the cinema and other modern media, presenting one of the particular challenges to the Church in this generation. For many of us this is made more difficult by the nature of our upbringing as Christians. We were grounded in the doctrinal content of the Gospel, and rightly so; but sadly few of us were taught to cope with our emotions; rather we were taught to suppress them ('feelings ain't facts') and to treat our bodily desires with suspicion. We then discover a medium which speaks primarily to the body and emotions and do not know how to cope with it. But our salvation in Christ is salvation for the whole man; body, mind, emotions and spirit. Discernment and walking in the Spirit are for every part of our make-up. Potentially we are equipped in Christ to handle Pop music. In itself it is neutral, and a vital contemporary means of communication, and the devil does not have all the good Pop music. Man is both fallen and in the image of God, and both of these aspects appear in Pop.

Pop in the seventies is in a vacuum; in terms of a message it has no clear sense of direction. Musically the main contents of the seventies Pop 'pie' are as follows: The re-emergence of fan mania over 'teeny-bop' idols (Donny Osmond, David Cassidy etc.)

Glitter, glam and show-biz Rock (Gary Glitter, Marc Bolan, The Sweet, etc.)

Stylized 'Art' Rock (David Bowie, Roxy Music, Alice Cooper, Sparks, etc., often with an ethos of decadence)

Nostalgia – the re-release of many past hits, the revival of Rock 'n' Roll, and the re-creation of past styles (eg by Roy Wood and Wizzard)

Good-time Rock music (by the Faces, Bad Company, and many American Country Rock bands)

Singer song-writers trying to work out their own philosophy of life (Joni Mitchell)

Groups of highly-advanced technical and musical ability, often using the new electronic synthesizers, etc. (Yes, Emerson Lake and Palmer, Mahavishnu Orchestra etc.)

Ballads, Soul music, Reggae and many other styles.

Parents should listen to discover their children's particular tastes. They should be aware of the danger areas (such as the way Alice Cooper plays on violence, Bowie on bisexuality, the fact that the Osmonds are devoted Mormons, and the fact that the Mahavishnu Orchestra play 'electric Hinduism'). But also they should look out for the many true statements about the heart and needs of man and the state of the world. To give you some help, a list of suggested reading and listening is given below. Above all, so ground your children in the Scriptures and in an understanding of salvation for the whole man, that they can face the special temptations of their own day and still enjoy that which has beauty and truth.

SUGGESTED READING
Art and the Bible, Francis Schaeffer (Hodder & Stoughton)

Modern Art and the Death of a Culture (the short section on music and the final chapters), Professor Rookmaaker (IVP)

Occasional copies of Melody Maker, New Musical Express, Let it Rock, etc.

SUGGESTED LISTENING
Rock 'n' Roll Shoes, from the LP *Rock of Ages* by The Band (on the nature of Pop music)

Why should the Devil have all the Good Music, from the LP *Only Visiting this Planet*, by Larry Norman

Court and Spark LP by Joni Mitchell

Quadrophenia LP by The Who

Ziggie Stardust and the Spiders from Mars LP by David Bowie

Dark Side of the Moon by Pink Floyd

The Inner Mounting Flame LP by the Mahavishnu Orchestra